M000036477

Dear Friend:

You may have noticed that this book is put together differently than most other quality paperbacks. The page you are reading, for instance, along with the back page, is glued to the cover. And when you open the book the spine "floats" in back of the pages. But there's nothing wrong with your book. These features allow us to produce what is known as a detached cover, specifically designed to prevent the spine from cracking even after repeated use. A state-of-the-art binding technology known as OtaBind® is used in the manufacturing of this and all Health Communications, Inc. books.

HCI has invested in equipment and resources that ensure the books we produce are of the highest quality, yet remain affordable. At our Deerfield Beach headquarters, our editorial and art departments are just a few steps from our pressroom, bindery and shipping facilities. This internal production enables us to pay special attention to the needs of our readers when we create our books.

Our titles are written to help you improve the quality of your life. You may find yourself referring to this book repeatedly, and you may want to share it with family and friends who can also benefit from the information it contains. For these reasons, our books have to be durable and, more importantly, user-friendly.

OtaBind® gives us these qualities. Along with a crease-free spine, the book you have in your hands has some other characteristics you may not be aware of:

- Open the book to any page and it will lie flat, so you'll never have to worry about losing your place.
- You can bend the book over backwards without damage, allowing you to hold it with one hand.
- The spine is 3-5 times stronger than conventional perfect binding, preventing damage even with rough handling.

This all adds up to a better product for our readers—one that will last for years to come. We stand behind the quality of our books and guarantee that, if you're not completely satisfied, we'll replace the book or refund your money within 30 days of purchase. If you have any questions about this guarantee or our bookbinding process, please feel free to contact our customer service department at 1-800-851-9100.

We hope you enjoy the quality of this book, and find understanding, insight and direction for your life in the information it provides.

**Health Communications, Inc.®**

3201 S.W. 15th Street
Deerfield Beach, FL 33442-8190
(305) 360-0909

Peter Vegso
President

# A YEAR
# OF
# KINDNESS

*A Year Of*

# Kindness

♥ ♥ ♥ ♥ ♥

### 365 Ways To
### Spread Sunshine

Hanoch McCarty & Meladee McCarty

**Health Communications, Inc.**
**Deerfield Beach, Florida**

Publisher:  Health Communications, Inc.
            3201 S.W. 15th Street
            Deerfield Beach, Florida 33442-8190

*Cover design by Lawna L. Oldfield*
*Cover cross-stitch by Debra B. Patterson*

To my mother, Laura Spiess, whose life has been filled with many challenges to which she has unfailingly responded with kindness, compassion and a gentle spirit. To have such a teacher has been my treasure and a shining beacon.

— *Meladee McCarty*


To Leona Green, my dear, dear friend, who reaches out to the world in kindness and love and establishes kinship and unity with such a panoply of others! Leona has truly been my mentor, demonstrating acceptance and forgiveness and breadth of her loving kindness.

— *Hanoch McCarty*

# *Acknowledgments*

We gratefully acknowledge the following friends, colleagues, helpers and family members for their contributions of ideas, time, energy, suggested improvements and also for their forbearance in listening to us when we were overflowing with the topic and just had to tell them another idea.

Particularly, we'd like to mention Macallister Dodds and Stephanie Dodds, our children, who listened and lived with two mad authors and forgave us for the many times we were taken away from them by our commitment to write this book. And Shayna Liora Hinds and Ethan Robert Rand McCarty, our grown children, whose support was just as present. Even though we're separated by many miles, their ideas and examples helped form our thinking. We've been blessed four times over by these special people.

A special mention must be made of Carolee Dunegin, a friend and a great, joyous helper with Grandma and with almost everything else. Her upbeat attitude and her world's greatest lemon bars have contributed much to our work!

We'd also like to acknowledge a raft of great kindness mentors: Holly Heine, Carol Hall, Karen McArthur, Len Leis, Esther Schultz, Florence Brown, Jeanette Jacobson, Adam Bendell, Julie Wolf, Joanne Clark, Mary Jane Cross, Harriet Doyle, Paula Simpfenderfer, Bill and Ann Seibert. Suzanne and Sidney Simon, Becky Smith, Lori Smith, June Mattingly, Cheryl Trujillo, Michael and Jacqueline Wenger, Janice Blackwill, Donna Auwater, Joy Schindler, Anne Quinn, Karen

Sweet, Beth McNett, Fred and Ann Richards, Miriam and Ron Hinds and always, the incredible A. Gringa Parnussa and Victor Schmenge.

Finally, our thoughtful and understanding editor, Christine Belleris, has brought a great spirit, great suggestions and much penetrating feedback. Her patience and strength have been our great resources. Thanks also to Pat Boyd, copy editor extraordinaire, whose long hours spent polishing our manuscript most certainly left her bleary-eyed.

# *January*

*S*mile and make eye contact with everyone you meet. You'll find people beaming back at you. In a small but perceptible way, you'll have made the world a better place.

# *January*

2

*O*ffer a shoulder to lean
on and a listening ear to someone
who needs a friend. When comfort
is given and a burden shared,
the road ahead seems
shorter.

*January*

*3*

$\mathscr{P}$at someone on the
back for a job well done—or for a
good honest try. Acknowledgment and
recognition makes both of you feel
good—and ready for yet more
positive things to be done.

# January

## 4

*S*ay "Thank you" in as many
ways as you can, for small things as
well as large favors. Everyone wants to
feel appreciated and valued—and
thank-yous are much
underrated.

# *January*

*5*

*G*ive an impromptu kiss
to someone you love. It sends the
message, "I love you for what you
do and who you are to me."

# January

**6**

*G*ive warm hugs—
you can tell if one is welcome.
And remember that a hug is often
worth a thousand words or even
a thousand deeds.

# *January*

*7*

*S*ay, "You look wonderful!"
and mean it. A positive self-image
makes everyone happier and
more productive.

# January

8

*R*ub a tired back—
and ask for a rub in return.
A back rub can make a trying
and dreary job seem
easy.

# January

**9**

*P*rovide a hot cup of
coffee for a repairperson
on a freezing day.

# January

**10**

*W*histle when you suddenly
feel down or play cheery music
if you're blue. It's a way of
letting a cheerful composer
become a friend.

# January

**11**

*K*eep within the speed limit.
You'll save gasoline
— and lives.

# *January*

**12**

*S*ay "Good morning" with
enthusiasm, even if it isn't one.
A positive outlook has
a way of being
contagious.

# January

## 13

*W*rite a caring letter to
an old friend. Old friends are worth
remembering and connections
can be kept alive by your
thoughtfulness.

# January

### 14

*S*urprise someone with a
phone call, and let him know he
matters to you in many
positive ways.

# January

### 15

*V*olunteer to do the dishes
or take out the trash. Your loved
one will appreciate the
additional support.

# January

## 16

$\mathcal{P}$ay your bills cheerfully.
Taking care of your responsibilities
is a kind way of reducing
unnecessary stress in
your life.

# January

**17**

*G*ive a party.
You'll be sure to lighten
everyone's post-holiday blues—
as well as your own.

# January

## 18

*M*eet your obligations
cheerfully. Negativity models
discouragement. Reframing the
negative into a positive
gives you hope.

# January

*19*

*T*ake the opportunity
to change the routine of daily
chores and put love into them for your
partner. Leave a note saying,
"There's more kindness
coming, beware!"

# January

## 20

*P*erk up someone's
day with a joke or a funny
story. A smile increases
your face value.

# January

**21**

$\mathcal{S}$how your appreciation
and consideration for your coworkers
by making coffee when the pot
is empty. Serve it with
a smile.

# January

## 22

*S*ave newspaper clippings
and pass them on to show you care
about others' concerns and others'
interests: help-wanted ads for the job
hunter and perhaps some
recipes for the chef.

# January

23

*W*rite an encouraging
letter to the editor of the local
paper. He'll be glad to
know his work is
valued.

# January

24

*T*ake Grandma and Grandpa
out to lunch at their favorite restaurant.
Celebrate them for the many lessons
they've taught you.

# *January*

*25*

$\mathcal{S}$how interest in
your friends' interests. Abandon
the contest of who gets heard.
Let it be your kindness today
to simply be the listener.

# January

**26**

*T*oday is a good day to be sensitive to a friend's disappointments or challenges. Don't bring up sore subjects in conversation unless they speak about them first.

# January

27

Send a letter of
appreciation to someone in public
office. You will encourage her at
what is often a thankless job
and help your agenda
as well.

# *January*

28

*W*ave and smile at a
parking enforcement officer.
He's really doing the community
a favor by keeping traffic flowing
so you can find a parking space
when you need one.

# January

**29**

*U*se up only one parking space.
Someone else will be coming
along and need the one
you might have
blocked.

# January

### 30

*P*ay your bills promptly.
You'll spare your
creditor a lot of worry
and trouble.

# January

**31**

*G*ive clothes you don't
wear to a needy person or to
an agency that'll pass them on.
Remember what your mother
taught you about sharing.

# February

**1**

*P*ay attention to positive news
and pass it on. Ask your local
TV station to do the same;
suggest that the late-night news
end on a positive note.

# February

**2**

$\mathcal{B}$uy the wine and cheese
your sweetheart likes and serve
them with a flair — with the TV turned
to "off." Feed the soul with
a little romance.

# February

3

*R*emember that faultfinding is
unlikely to cause a change; say something
nice instead. People grow more when
noticed for their strengths rather
than their weaknesses.

*February*

*4*

*C*onsider a different
point of view, remembering
that the person you disagree with has
put just as much into his idea as you
put into yours. The chance of
coming to an agreement will
be much greater.

# February

5

*L*end a favorite book
and don't worry about getting
it back. Buy another book instead.
Consider your loan an important
gift of literature.

## February

**6**

*W*hether it's cards or
racquetball or something else,
enjoy the game and let your opponent
enjoy it, too. Don't play as though
your life depends on it; play
as though your love
depends on it.

# February

7

*R*eturn a friend's favorite
book and show your appreciation:
write a note or invite him to dinner to
discuss it. Talking about a book
together can add a lot to
understanding one another.

# February

8

*T*oss a ball to a little kid—or
to a big one. You'll find that
the joy of play is greatly
underrated.

# February

9

*H*elp someone find a
solution instead of giving advice.
Even more valuable than the immediate
solution will be the know-how
and self-confidence
you instill.

# February

**10**

*T*ake a box of homemade
cookies to work and leave them
unobtrusively by the coffee machine.
Leave a note saying they come
from the Phantom
of Kindness.

# February

## 11

$\mathcal{V}$isit an elderly shut-in —
and show an interest in her life.
Ask her to tell old stories and *listen*, and
ask for more. Older people have
much to give, and they
want to give it.

# February

**12**

*F*orgive an old grudge
and do it freely. Let the other
person know it's over and done with.
Then wonder at the new closeness
that opens up.

# February

### 13

$G$o out of your way to talk
to a lonely child, but do more listening
than talking. On another day tell
him of your lonely childhood
moments and how you have
survived them.

# February

*14*

Write a love poem for
your sweetheart. Print it out
on parchment paper and frame it.
Read it to your love by
candlelight.

# *February*

**15**

*L*augh at a boring joke.
After all, the person is
trying to make contact;
so help him.

# *February*

## 16

*S*ay,
"You're really wonderful!"
and make sure you mean it. Everyone
has some wonderful characteristics.
If you'll notice, they will
flower.

# February

**17**

*Everyone is beautiful, except we
lose the eyes to see it.*

—Jean McCarty

Tell her she's beautiful—
or tell him he's handsome. It's up to
you, for beauty is in the eye
of the beholder.

## February

### 18

*T*ake some children to
a park or to the zoo—or take
the child in yourself if there aren't any
other kids around. There's much to
be enjoyed and learned.

# February

19

*A*sk a neighbor to join
you on a trip to a museum. You'll be
surprised at how much there is to
whet your curiosity. And how much
more you can enjoy it with
someone else!

# *February*

## 20

*I*nvite some children to
play in the snow or at the shore if
you live in a warm-weather state.
Throw snowballs or beachballs;
make hot chocolate or
pink lemonade.

# February

**21**

*S*erve breakfast in bed to
your partner or to anyone handy.
Whether the mood is to be glamorous
or comfy-cozy, you can use
your imagination to set
the scene.

# *February*

**22**

*M*ake homecoming special
for your partner. Greet your love
with soothing music, soft lighting and
a warm greeting. Serve wine and
have pleasant conversation.

# February

**23**

Clean the house for Mom and Dad.
It's a thoughtful way of returning
their many gifts of love
and support.

# February

**24**

$\mathcal{S}$hare a dream. Tell it with
your full artistry. Don't be afraid
to be corny or sentimental.
Place your faith and trust
in your listener.

# February

**25**

*T*ake a walk with your
partner or someone else and
leave the Walkman™ and cellular phone
at home. You'll discover each
other all over again.

# *February*

**26**

*B*e eyes and ears for friends
who want to find something special—
an item for a collection, a certain food or
whatever it is they want. Knowing and
meeting another's need is a big part
of being a friend.

# *February*

27

*A*dopt a stray cat
or let a stray cat adopt you.
Everyone needs a home. And a cat
to be loved will make
yours happier.

*February*

**28**

*B*e there today for a child
who needs a caring adult and lots
of attention. If you don't know one, call
the Big Brothers/Big Sisters office
nearest you or phone your local
school district.

# *Leap Day*

*C*heck yourself if you're
about to say too much about a
friend: guard confidences with care.
You can't help someone who is in
trouble if you're not one
to be trusted.

# March

1

*T*ry understanding a teenager.
It may be difficult, but keep trying.
And remember, you don't have
to agree with someone to
understand him.

## *March*

*2*

*T*ry to understand
someone who thinks or behaves
in a way that is different from you.
You're bound to find common
ground if only you'll try.

# March

**3**

$\mathcal{S}$queeze the toothpaste
tube from the bottom if it matters to
someone else. If not, perhaps you
should give up caring about
such small stuff.

*March*

*4*

*R*elay an overheard compliment. You'll make someone value himself a little more, and you may be introducing him to an unknown friend.

## *March*

**5**

*F*orget a negative
remark you have overheard.
Negative comments and criticisms
have negative results.

# March

6

*L*et someone ahead of
you in line. The little reduction
in stress that you give may
make a big difference.

# *March*

**7**

*A*cknowledge your mistakes.
If you've done or said something
wrong, just say so. Everyone is
reassured in knowing that the
other guy goofs up, too.

*March*

*L*et someone know
he was right. Do this with a
good heart and a loving
tone of voice.

# March

**9**

*T*oday use all the courtesies
that used to be so common—please,
thank you, pardon me—and now
seem so rare. A little courtesy
goes a long way.

# *March*

**10**

*H*ave "Yes" ever ready
in your heart. Embrace life!
Have laughter and liveliness
always on your lips.

## March

### 11

$\mathcal{T}$each your children or a neighbor how to change a tire—before they have a flat. Do it on a nice, sunny day so they'll have the skills needed on a dark, rainy night. Put a flashlight, some flares and a set of jumper cables in each child's trunk.

# March

**12**

*B*e alert to a skill
you have that others may need.
You might offer to type a business
letter for a friend or wrap a
parcel if his fingers
are all thumbs.

# *March*

## 13

$\mathscr{P}$itch in to break the logjam
of someone suffering from writer's block.
A simple question about the project
may suddenly restore the flow.
Or a simple expression of interest
may perform a special magic.

*March*

14

*E*xplain patiently when
someone just doesn't get what you
are trying to convey. Write it down or
draw a picture. You'll both be
smiling when the light
dawns at last.

# March

15

*H*old your tongue if you're
about to tell "a hard truth" to someone.
Consider whether it's really truth
at all, and make sure it's not a
cruelty clothed in the rented
costume of kindness.

# *March*

**16**

*B*e patient and gentle
with sadness. The kindness is to
remember that grieving is a process
and not just a feeling.

# March

## 17

$\mathcal{S}$end a friend a shamrock plant
for St. Patrick's Day. Include a note
that says, "When you come home,
someone will be rooting
for you."

# March

## 18

*L*ook about you and
notice the small problems of others
that you can solve in an unobtrusive way.
In the supermarket, reach the top-shelf
item for a short person or open a
door for someone laden with
too many parcels.

# *March*

*19*

*P*ractice calm.
Deliberately build into your
day quiet times of listening to music
or watching the birds. When calm
emanates from you, it dissolves
others' stress.

# *March*

20

*A*cknowledge the people
whose service you too often take
for granted. Say thanks to your letter
carrier and the trash collector.

## March

*21*

$\mathcal{P}$ay attention to a child who
seems to be left out. Talk to him, listen
to him; explain something he seems
to be wondering about. How many
times have you seen a child who looks
lost—who needs to belong! Make
sure there is one less child
who is lost today.

## March

### 22

*R*emember that others
have the same boring chores as you
—and while you're at it, knock off
another's chore as well as yours.
Change a printer cartridge
at the office or mow a
neighbor's grass.

# *March*

**23**

*S*hare your umbrella
and be willing to give it away.
It may be returned by a stranger
who turns into a friend.

# March

## 24

*M*ake up a "care and love"
package for a friend or homeless person.
Include some fun things and some food
for thought. These are vitamins for the
spirit. Ask your family to help
plan the package's contents.

# *March*

**25**

*C*arry a warm sweater,
jacket or blanket in your car
for anyone you see who is cold and
homeless.  You will be giving
not only warmth but
also heart.

## *March*

**26**

*W*hen you remember a
favorite poem, think of friends
who would enjoy it: write it out neatly
and mail it with a note. Shared beauty
seems somehow doubled.

# *March*

**27**

*L*eave little love notes for
your partner or any family member.
Leave lots—on a desk or a dashboard,
and especially in odd places.
It's unlikely you'll say "I love you"
too often.

# March

## 28

*S*end a letter ahead to
a hotel where your sweetheart
or a friend will be staying. It will
carry not only a personal greeting
but also the comfort
of home.

## *March*

*29*

*B*e quiet when
someone is watching a favorite
TV show. His private interests
are as important to him as
yours are to you.

# *March*

**30**

*G*ive a cutting from your garden to a friend or give one from a house plant. He'll be delighted by the new variety and probably return the favor. A rose is not just a rose.

# *March*

**31**

*S*hare a beautiful
sunset with a friend. The habit
of looking and really seeing is
a gift worth sharing.

*April*

1

*D*eliberately put
a little humor into your life.
Combine play and work today, and
every day, for humor connects
us with others.

# April

## 2

*S*ay "I love you"
often. Don't wait to be asked.
Have you said all the "I love you's"
that you need to? Write a note.
Make a call.

*April*

3

*R*ent a cassette of a
funny movie and share it
with someone whose spirits are
dragging. Your caring, as well
as the movie, may change his
whole point of view.

# *April*

*4*

*C*arry cough drops or
mints in your pocket or handbag.
You'll provide welcome
relief for someone
in need.

*April*

5

*G*ive a soft answer to
a hostile question. Not only are
two needed to tango but
also to fight.

# April

### 6

*T*oday come up with
as many ways as you can to say
"I'm sorry." Brainstorm with a friend
or colleague. Talk about the benefits
you'd get from a creative,
sincere apology.

*April*

7

*E*ncourage a youngster.
It may be that nothing stands
in his or her way but self-doubt —
and abilities can't grow unless
they are tested.

# April

**8**

*T*alk to someone who
is facing a failure about your
failures and about how you have
overcome them. Be a distributor
of hope today.

*April*

9

*R*esolve not to
magnify small problems. Your own
choice of language affects how you begin
to see your situation; the bigger the
language, the bigger the problem.
Choose to use the language
of hope.

*April*

*10*

*L*eave negative
things unsaid. Don't shoot
from the lip.

# April

## 11

*Today is a gift; tomorrow is only a promise.*

—Anonymous

*G*ive the gift of time.
Renegotiate and reprioritize to make the
time for the people and activities
you cherish the most.

*April*

*12*

*W*rite problems down
on paper. Take time to think things
through and make changes if necessary.
It's a kindness to yourself
to find clarity.

*April*

*13*

*A*sk for help from a
friend or counselor if a problem
has you stuck. Allow yourself the
right to get help by sharing
your burden.

*April*

*14*

*F*orgive an injustice.
Work with another person to explore
the acceptable alternatives. Sometimes a
person's unjust or unfair behavior
comes from not seeing what else
they might have done.

*April*

*15*

*B*e fully present when
someone else is talking: concentrate
on him and *really* listen.
Everyone wants to be acknowledged
as being—and as being worth
listening to as well.

*April*

*16*

*E*xamine your demands
on others. Give some of them up.
Fulfill your demands yourself instead
of insisting that someone else
take care of them.

*April*

*17*

*F*ind the funny side of a situation. Be a "fun resource" today: a person others can always count on for a smile and a new, humorous way to look at things.

# April

## 18

*J*ust do it if you feel
like blowing your top — after you
have parked your car in a quiet,
safe place. Just scream. You'll be
sparing some innocent victim
your pent-up rage.

*April*

*19*

*L*augh when the
joke is on you. We all take
tumbles from time to time;
so join the crowd.

*April*

**20**

*A friend is someone who knows your song
and sings it to you when you forget.*

—Anonymous

*H*elp someone
remember the good he's done,
the talent he possesses and
his value to you.

*April*

*21*

*E*ncourage a beginner to try something that has an element of risk in it. Help her prepare so that the risk is reduced. Support her through the boring practice and inevitable mistakes. Be a mentor if she needs one.

*April*

*22*

*T*angibly express your
gratitude for a past favor. If someone
once gave you a "leg up" when you
needed help getting started, resolve to
pass on the favor. Be that "leg-up"
person for someone as soon
as you can.

*April*

*23*

*R*ead something
uplifting to someone. As you
read it, listen to it
yourself.

*April*

*24*

*D*o what you
value, and value what you do.
Your integrity will be a
beacon to others.

*April*

*25*

*A*lways carry a camera with
you and jump at the chance to catch
kindness and caring people in action.
Make copies of the photos and
send them to the kind folks
on your film.

*April*

26

*C*onnect and reduce the
gaps between yourself and others.
Share your feelings and thoughts.
Take the risk of
closeness.

*April*

27

*If* you see litter on the
sidewalk, pick it up instead of walking
over it. You know you didn't drop it,
but you have the power to pick it up and
make your world more
beautiful today.

*April*

*28*

*B*e yourself.
What a sense of security
you'll give to others who need
reassurance that "real"
people do exist.

# April

**29**

*P*oint out
the beauty and wonder of
nature to those you love. Stop
long enough to enjoy it
yourself.

*April*

*30*

*W*alk tall.
Let your pride show in
your posture and the twinkle
in your eyes.

*May*

1

*A*void towering over people.
Pull up a chair to a wheelchair; get
down to the level of a child.
Don't make people look up to you:
be physically as well as
otherwise equal.

## May

**2**

*E*njoy a starry night
and ask someone to join you.
Stretch out in a lounge chair
or lie on the grass—
and just wonder.

# May

3

Say "I love you"
in different languages.
*Je t'aime. Te amo. Ich liebe dich.*

# *May*

**4**

*Look at each person you meet as a Person In Progress . . . in the process of growing and changing . . . trying their best to get better. Then, look in the mirror and see another Person In Progress.*

—Carl Rogers

*L*et go of the urge to be critical to someone.

*May*

5

*T*alk about your gratitude
for the good things that come your
way—an unexpected phone call or
even, sometimes, a rainy day.
You'll be encouraging the joy
of gratitude in others.

*May*

*6*

*H*um out loud the song
in your heart. Invite others
to join you.

*May*

7

*D*rop a dollar bill on
the sidewalk or in a hallway. Write a
note on it: "A gift from the Kindness
Revolution." Take pleasure in
imagining the little "extra"
it will buy.

*May*

*8*

$\mathcal{E}$ase someone's
embarrassment at a blunder
by telling of some such faux pas
of your own. You may end up
laughing together and turn an
embarassing moment into
a treasured memory.

*May*

*9*

*B*e charitable to
yourself about mistakes.
Do unto yourself as you
do unto others.
You're human, too!

*May*

*10*

$\mathscr{T}$ake someone on a surprise
outing: get tickets for a ball game,
reserve a window table at a country inn.
Plan extra little surprises
along the way.

# *May*

*11*

*W*hen the circus comes to town,
be there—and take someone with you.
Buy a dozen red foam clown noses
and wear one for the performance.
Give the rest out to your friends or other
audience members in your section.

*May*

*12*

*A*sk someone for a
favor that acknowledges a
special talent she has: ask for help
with your flower garden or
with your computer.

*May*

*13*

*G*ive a gift that doesn't
seem like a gift, but more like sharing.
Make a double batch of cookies
or buy two flashlights for
the price of one.

*May*

*14*

*If you don't cuddle, you'll curdle.*

—Jess Lair

*N*ever miss an opportunity
to be affectionate to
your loved ones.

# *May*

**15**

*L*eave a rose under
someone's windshield wiper.
Let the thought of your gift of
beauty enrich his day.

# *May*

16

*O*n the highway,
wave to the bored children
in the back of the car ahead;
you'll see them smile
and wave back.

# May

17

*T*hink about the
rewarding aspects of your job;
add to the satisfaction by doing it with
your full artistry and commitment.
It's a kindness to model
quiet competence.

*May*

*18*

$\mathcal{S}$end an uplifting quotation
every day to someone who's despairing.
The persistence of your loving
kindness will help your
friend believe again.

# *May*

## 19

*S*end a get-well wish to a
sick friend every day for as long as
need be; take pictures of people and
places you both love, and write
your messages on the back
of each picture.

## May

**20**

$\mathcal{D}$raw a hot, soothing bubble
bath for the one you love. Light scented
candles and leave a note by the tub
that reads, "No one holds a candle to you
in my eyes. You're the one who
makes me warm."

*May*

21

*W*atch for coupons
offering services your friends need
and pass them on. Add kind or funny
notes or coupons for services
you'd be willing to offer.

*May*

**22**

*D*o something with the happy
memories of vacations spent with
friends. Dig out old maps and postcards,
snapshots and playbills; make a
collage and share it
with them.

# May

## 23

*If* a friend is feeling grief,
be with him or her. Don't worry
about finding the right words; your
presence is the most important
act of kindness.

*May*

24

*H*ave faith in yourself
and someone you know. The act of
expecting a miracle — really acting as if
it's going to happen and recognizing
it when it comes — that is the gift
that transforms helpless
into hopeful.

## May

### 25

*Surrender to the inevitability*
*of your success!*

—Dr. Frank Ciccone

$\mathcal{B}$elieve in yourself.
Your belief in yourself will have
many benefits and you will be a
model to everyone you know.

*May*

26

*L*eave that full briefcase
at the office; resolve to go to work
early in the morning to sort it out.
It's a kindness to devote the evening
to your family and friends
—and to yourself.

*May*

27

*C*reate a dinner chain
for someone who is suffering a loss
from death or divorce. When a social
pattern is broken, good friendships
can fade. Help prompt others
to remember their part
in the chain.

*May*

*28*

*U*rge the personnel manager
at your office to provide a counseling
service. It's a great kindness to recognize
that employees are people, not
just "functions."

*May*

*29*

*K*eep alive the memory of
a beautiful person. Gather books
significant to her and donate them to
the local library. If you prefer, plant a
memorial tree or create a small
fund to do good works in
your friend's name.

*May*

*30*

*M*ake the world safer for
children with your commitment to
kindness. Join in any efforts
to fight child abuse or to
find a missing child.

## May

31

*R*emember a retiree who's
alone and too frail to take care of
his home. Set up a fund to give
him housecleaning service
once a month.

# June

**1**

*C*ollect cartoons that make you laugh and share them with your friends and colleagues. Start a cartoon file and save favorites, especially those that illustrate or help bring humor to some aspects of your work or family life.

*June*

2

*D*raw mustaches on the
pictures of famous people in the
morning newspaper. Blacken in their
teeth and hair, draw glasses and that old
favorite, an arrow through the head.
Leave the paper for your
family to enjoy.

# June

3

$\mathscr{B}$uy some funny books and
keep them near your phone for those
seemingly endless minutes when you are
kept "on hold." It's an easy and
pleasant way to avoid
a bad temper.

## June

### 4

$\mathcal{P}$ack a "humor and fun kit" for your car. Include bubbles, noisemakers and other whimsical items. Instead of blowing your top when traffic grinds to a halt, you can blow bubbles into the wind.

*June*

*5*

*M*ake the most of a far-away friend's short layover at your local airport or train station. Surprise your pal with a basket lunch. Complete the package with flowers and your favorite taped music.

*June*

6

*S*end a care package
to someone who is far from home.
Include a nice card or letter and some of
their favorite special treats to nibble
on while they read your greeting.
Slip in playful photos of
friends and family.

# June

7

$\mathcal{G}$lue a special message,
caption, photo or newspaper clipping
to a piece of sturdy cardboard.
Cut the cardboard in jigsaw puzzle pieces
and send one piece each day or week
to a special person in your life.

*June*

*8*

*M*ake a collection of
an old friend's favorite tunes on
tape and send it to him. Add a message
from you at the end reminding him that
although far away, he's still
close at heart.

# June

**9**

*W*hen you travel away
from home, leave love notes for
your family to open each day
while you're gone.

*June*

*10*

*S*end your mother flowers on
your birthday with a loving, thank-you
note that reads, "If it weren't for you,
I wouldn't even have a birthday!
I love you very much."

# June

## 11

*It is those times when we least deserve a hug and support when we need them the most.*
—Glennis Weatherall

*P*ut some kind of temporary closure on a disagreement you can't resolve. Give a hug; express your faith it will be worked out.

*June*

*12*

*O*ffer a cold glass of
ginger ale to a worker on a hot day.
Be alert to your chances to lift
someone's spirits.

*June*

*13*

*I*gnore a rude remark.
Remember that this person's rudeness
speaks loudly about his feelings
and experiences and says
nothing about you.

*June*

*14*

*A*void saying "I told you so."
A learning experience belongs to the
person who had it. "I told you so's"
create more anger than
wisdom.

## June

### 15

$\int$houlder a blame once in
a while, even if you don't own it.
Your shoulders will become
stronger and your spirit
will grow, too!

# June

### 16

*L*et someone win an
argument. The proof is in the
pudding, not the recipe.

# June

## 17

*O*n the grocery list,
write the ingredients of a favorite
dish and add, "I love this special meal
and the love you put into
making it."

# June

## 18

$\mathcal{D}$o the laundry for your
family and stuff their underwear
with love notes. To really get a giggle,
include papier-mâché fruit.

# June

## 19

*W*hen your loved one is
traveling, call her hotel in advance
of her arrival and leave a loving message.
It's nice to be greeted so warmly
when you're tired and far
from home.

# *June*

**20**

*L*earn the sign language for
"I love you." You'll begin to learn
a new, beautiful language.

# June

**21**

*T*ake some plastic helium balloons to the park and give them away to the children you see there. Delight in their joy.

## June

### 22

*If* you can't afford to buy
a friend or loved one a gift for his
birthday or other special occasion, make
a love collage. Include artwork, pictures,
shells, silly sayings and lots of TLC.
Your gift will be a
treasured keepsake.

## June

### 23

*Everybody has some beautiful aspect, talent
or quality. If you look for it, you'll find it.
If you acknowledge them for it,
they'll be forever grateful.*

— Jean McCarty

*L*ook for something beautiful
in one person each day.

## June

### 24

*F*ill a pretty jar with a
variety of nuts and circle it with
a ribbon. Attach a note that says,
"I'm nuts about you."

*June*

*25*

*P*raise your spouse and family
members in front of others.
It never hurts.

*June*

26

*B*e a good listener.
Look directly in the eyes of the
one who's speaking and listen for the
meaning of what is said. You'll find
yourself saying "Yes" or "Exactly" —
or perhaps, "No, of course not."
You'll connect.

# June

## 27

$C$arry tissues in your purse
or glove compartment. They'll come
in handy when someone sheds a
tear or spills a drink.

*June*

*28*

*R*aise your spirits and
those of others by being thankful.
Start a Thankful Journal and
keep a daily record of what you're
thankful for. Read it on the days
when things look gray.

# June

## 29

*C*hoose to ignore the
things that will rile you up.
Forgive even if you
can't forget.

*June*

*30*

*R*each out and touch someone.
Shake hands and affirm your connection
by lightly touching a companion in
conversation. Studies show that
being touched is pleasant
and relaxing.

# July

1

*R*eframe negative thoughts:
The glass is half full; it's not half empty.
You have passed four exams;
you have fallen short on only one.
You will encourage not only yourself
but also others.

*July*

2

*K*now yourself; believe in
yourself. If someone finds it necessary
to put you down, whose problem is it?
It's a problem of his, which you
can choose to ignore — and you can
avoid a damaging quarrel.

*July*

*3*

*H*elp your boss.
She's trying to respond not
only to demands from above but also
other people's personal needs—and she
has needs herself. Try to see what her
needs are and support her.

## July

4

$\mathcal{D}$ress up in your best red, white and
blue and lead the neighborhood
children in a patriotic
songfest.

# July

**5**

*Genuine humor is always kindly
and gracious. It points out the weakness
of humanity, but shows no contempt
and leaves no sting.*

— Anonymous

Remember that the weakness
you find so funny in another
may also be yours.

# July

**6**

*Take your job seriously and
yourself lightly.*

— Joel Goodman

$\mathscr{P}$ut a stop to compulsive
strivings for perfection—it's not
quite human and thus less than welcome
in the workplace or anywhere else.

# July

7

*A*dd a humorous item
to the agenda of an office or
family meeting. Levity is a friendly
antidote for self-importance.

*July*

*8*

*T*hrow a curve at the
people who take themselves too
seriously at business meetings.
Serve ice cream cones
with sprinkles.

*July*

**9**

*B*uy a pass for public transportation and keep it handy for a time when you see the need. It may be the ticket to a job for a person who's out of work.

# July

## 10

$\mathcal{R}$ecruit some neighborhood
kids to clean up graffiti. Not only
will the eyesore be gone, but the kids will
send out the message that they value
their own neighborhood.

*July*

*11*

*R*emove dangerous hazards
in the workplace—a dangling cord,
a wastebasket that should be somewhere
else. Caring for another's safety is
a sign that you care for him.

## July

12

*M*ind your own business; don't "chat" about personal information that others have confided. You'll preclude the kind of gossip that ends up doing harm.

# July

## 13

*T*ake the responsibility
for your own feelings rather than
laying the blame at someone
else's feet.

# July

## 14

*When I ignore my feelings, my
stomach keeps score.*

— Hanoch McCarty

*M*odel communication skills which
allow everyone to be heard and respected.
Use phrases that open discussion, such as:
"Tell me more . . ." or "Help
me understand . . ."

*July*

*15*

*E*ncourage coworkers to
bring in baby or early childhood
pictures of themselves for the bulletin
board. Have them include a funny quote
about how they viewed the world at
that age. Award prizes for the
most creative lines.

# July

**16**

*L*eave a thank-you note and
some refreshments for the nighttime
office cleaners. They must often
feel that no one knows
they exist.

# July

## 17

*V*olunteer to help — if only for
one day — at some kind of local shelter.
You'll be giving a welcome respite
to a tired worker — and you can
light the way for friends.

## July

### 18

$\mathcal{L}$et it be known that you're
willing to baby-sit in an emergency.
How often a single parent needs
a back-up to be able to visit
the doctor or attend to
important business!

*July*

*19*

*P*ut up a big sign at the office:
"No swearing, complaining or
gossiping allowed. Fine for violations:
$1.00 in the Staff Gaffe Fund can below."
Have a party with the proceeds.

*July*

*20*

$\mathscr{P}$ay for dinner for someone
who's clearly hungry but only ordering
coffee. Ask the waitress to tell
him it's on the house.

# July

## 21

*A*sk some coworkers to help
you decorate the staff lunchroom or
lounge to bring a bit of beauty
into every day.

# July

## 22

*T*ake some stuffed animals
to the children's ward at your local
hospital. Of course you'll be giving
comfort to the children—and you'll also
raise the spirits of the nurses
who hand them out.

# July

## 23

*L*eave Hershey's™ chocolate Hugs™ and Kisses™ on the desk of an office friend who has helped you out with a note saying, "Hugs and kisses to you for the support and professionalism you gave me with this project."

## July

*24*

*S*et up a discount coupon
resource at your neighborhood
senior center. Cover a box with attractive
paper and fill it with coupons for food
and toiletries. Ask visitors to join in
and also the seniors themselves.

*July*

*25*

*O*ffer an encouraging word
to someone who is tired of waiting—
perhaps for the doctor or for the bus.
This is a great time to practice
your listening skills.

*July*

26

*R*espect and value every
human you meet no matter how humble.
Say *Namaste* in spirit if not in words:
In Hindi it is shorthand for
"I salute the spirit of godliness
I see in you."

*July*

27

*H*elp others to lighten up.
Say, with a grin, "You're a short time
livin' and a long time gone."
Live this day fully
and lovingly.

*July*

*28*

*M*ake at least three affirmations
of other people per day. If you are in the
habit of appreciating people, it will
raise your awareness level of the
joyfulness in your own life.

# July

29

*A*ffirm your faith in the
institutions that support you—
your church or synagogue, your school
or college, and even your legislature.
Verbalize your faith; let
others know.

*July*

*30*

*T*ake joy and pleasure
in doing a favor. And let
the recipient enjoy
your joy.

*July*

*31*

*G*o beyond forgiving
yourself for a transgression.
Think about how you could have
done better; affirm your ability
to behave in a different way
on the next occasion.

# *August*

*1*

*D*onate blood.
You may just
save a life.

# August

2

*If we don't like the world we're in, there is always the option to create the world we desire via acts of kindness.*

—Meladee McCarty

*F*ind the good in every person, place and thing today. Jot down your feelings at day's end.

*August*

3

*N*ever give up on anybody.
Notice progress in them, however small.
Sharpen your perception; you may
see improvements she herself
has overlooked.

# August

4

$\mathcal{B}$e respectful of public servants. Thank them for helping and tell them you appreciate what they are doing. Brighten their day with a joke or pun and a warm smile. It recharges their batteries to full capacity, which helps their outlook and the service they give you.

# August

5

*L*ocate a lonely,
homebound person and
become his phone pal. Just tell
an overworked clergyman or rabbi
you want to be of help.

# August

**6**

$\mathcal{D}$on't go to bed mad;
don't leave on a trip on an
angry note. A door that you close
behind you may automatically
lock—but one loving word
will keep it ajar.

*August*

7

*The only one who cannot learn
is an expert.*

—Harry S. Truman

*C*hoose to be humble. When we
are full of ourselves, we cannot benefit
from what others have to give us.

# *August*

*8*

*G*ive others a chance to
give to you. We all need to feel
we have something to give
that is of value.

# *August*

*9*

*Always do what's right. It will please
some and astonish the rest.*

—Anonymous

Don't tolerate racist,
sexist, agist or homophobic talk
or slurs: gently but firmly refuse to
listen. Don't be an accomplice.

# August

## 10

*C*hoose not to label people.
Remember that hate is born of fear.
We can lower our level of fear by
building our understanding of
others who are different
from us.

*August*

*11*

*I*f you have children, love
and support them for who they are.
Build bridges between you; don't
distance yourself because of
their different lifestyle.

# August

## 12

*I*nvite someone you have met
from a different culture to join in
social gatherings with your friends.
Include a wide variety of people
into your social group.

# August

13

Work on your empathy skills.
Don't assume that a single parent is
doing something wrong or that
someone who is unemployed
has no ambition.

# August

## 14

*C*ontact at least one person
who has contributed something
important to your life and thank him.
Maybe your favorite teacher
or maybe an early boss.

# August

## 15

*N*egative criticisms beget
more criticisms. Stop the cycle.
Ask yourself, "Is what I'm about to say
likely to help this person grow?"

# August

## 16

*D*onate time; donate talent.
Take a wheelchair patient at a nursing
home for a spin out-of-doors;
get nursing home patients together
for a sing-along.

# August

**17**

*S*end a fax to a work associate
expressing thanks for his input,
his promptness or his
good humor.

# August

## 18

*R*isk letting people know you.
Share a personal talent or interest.
This opens the window into who
you are and how you think.

## August

**19**

$\mathcal{V}$ow to do something with a
friend you have always wanted to do,
but have never done: go on an adventure
to an exotic place, go skydiving or learn
how to sail. Call your friend today
and make a date for it to happen.

# August

## 20

*R*esolve not to make promises
unless you are sure you can keep them;
the sense of insecurity spawned by
broken promises can be traumatic.
Be someone who can be
counted on.

*August*

21

*D*evelop an ability that can
be helpful. Take a first aid course,
sign up for crisis intervention
training or volunteer for
a suicide hotline.

## August

**22**

$\mathcal{S}$pend an hour with someone
who is grieving. Bring a pot roast or
some flowers. This act of kindness is
never wasted, even if the results
aren't immediately visible.

*August*

*23*

*L*ook forward and say
"I can"; don't look backward and say
"I should have." Others will be
encouraged by your forward progress;
don't deaden their spirits, or your
own, with woeful regrets.

*August*

24

*I*nvite a friend to exercise
with you. Run, walk or take an aerobics
or yoga class together. Lower your
cholesterol and heighten your bonds of
friendship in one fell swoop.

*August*

*25*

*S*tart a sharing bookshelf
at your office. Encourage colleagues
to bring in their old books to share
with others. If you take a book,
leave one in its place.

# August

**26**

*L*ook actively in the daily
paper and on the TV screen for
news of acts of kindness. Pass on
the news to others that there
is actually goodness
going on.

# *August*

**27**

*G*et together a
Better Bumper-Sticker Brigade.
Make bumper stickers saying:
"I don't get mad, I get more loving."
"Kindness Happens."
"Give 'em Heaven."

# August

28

*C*opy this message on
a large batch of index cards:
"I wonder why we are not kinder than
we are. Kindness is so easy."
Leave the cards under windshield wipers.
There will be results.

# August

**29**

*H*ang a whisk broom
near your workplace or your desk.
Let it symbolically remind you to
tidy up—and not to leave
chores for others.

# August

## 30

*S*ay more than "Thank you"
at the end of a faxed request. Say
"Thank you for always being so prompt"
or "Thank you for that fine report
last week." Give specific
recognition.

*August*

*31*

*A*dd your company's motto
or mission statement to your faxes.
It reminds you and others that
you have values.

*September*

*P*lay a funny cassette on
your way to work instead of listening
to the news. Who says you have
to be informed about murder
and mayhem?

# September

**2**

*R*esolve to stop magnifying
small problems into big dilemmas.
Today focus on fixing the problem
instead of fixing the blame.

*September*

3

*G*ive yourself encouragement
to conquer workday stresses. Put a
mirror on your desk and, before each
challenging phone call, give yourself
a big smile. Fill yourself
with confidence.

*September*

*4*

*M*odel kind words.
Words that you have to eat
can be hard to swallow.

*September*

5

*Laughter is internal jogging.*
—Sidney Simon

*T*ell a joke or relate a
funny story to a friend or family
member who is sick. Humor—
more potent than drugs—will relax
him enough to sleep.

# *September*

**6**

*If I can stop one Heart from breaking /
I shall not live in vain / If I can ease
one Life the Aching / Or cool one pain /
Or help one fainting robin / Unto his nest
again / I shall not live in vain.*

— Emily Dickinson

*R*each for immortality by
doing a kindness today.

# September

7

*L*augh at an old joke.
Don't roll your eyes and sigh.
Don't interrupt and say you've heard
it before. And don't give away
the punch line.

*September*

*8*

$\mathcal{T}$ake time to really listen
to others. Fight to overcome
interruptions, distractions,
competitiveness and unsolicited
advice-giving. Simply lend
a concerned ear.

*September*

9

*B*ring a houseplant to
a new retiree who lives alone.
Even the small responsibility of caring
for it will help him to fill the void.
Suggest that he is now the
"Plant Manager."

*September*

10

*N*ever fire off an angry fax.
Let the angry ones sit for several
days until your anger
has cooled down.

*September*

*11*

*C*arry a "care kit" that
includes bandages, safety pins,
a comb and other odd bits.
A little handy help can avoid
embarrassment.

*September*

*12*

*R*emember that no position
on any issue is ever totally right or
totally wrong. Leave room for
negotiation; you're sure to
come nearer to the truth.

*September*

*13*

*O*ffer your seat to
someone who needs it on a
crowded bus or train or
at a meeting.

*September*

*14*

*P*ause and count to ten
before you vocalize an angry word.
This can break the anger cycle.

*September*

*15*

*W*hen you are driving,
let someone go ahead
of you in traffic.

*September*

16

$\mathcal{L}$et the other driver have
the parking spot that the person is
ready to kill for. You may save a
fender-bender, and you're sure to reduce
the person's hostility quotient.

# September

## 17

Swallow your pride.
Is it really more important to
be right than it is to
be happy?

## September

### 18

*F*orgive someone who
falls short of your expectations.
Consider that the other person may have
good reasons for his behavior. His idea
of what is right in the situation
may be quite different
from yours.

*September*

19

$\mathcal{P}$oke fun at the incongruities
in situations. What a relief for all and
an enlightenment to realize we can't
make sense of everything!

## September

### 20

*E*xpress your gratitude for something good that has come your way. You'll add to your appreciation and enjoyment of life; you'll help others to do the same.

*September*

*21*

$\mathcal{L}$ook at the errors of a
new employee as part of a learning
experience, not as a prognostication
that he will fail. Help him to
get it right.

*September*

22

*J*ump at the chance
to give credit when it is due.
For those embarrassed by public praise,
give private, or indirect praise:
"I like the way someone cleaned the
cabinet. Great job!"

# *September*

*23*

*V*olunteer to tutor an
immigrant in English and help
her to negotiate in a world that may
seem strange to her.

# September

*24*

Volunteer to read aloud
to children at your local library.
Help them to enjoy and
value books.

*September*

*25*

𝒫ush the "off" button on
the remote control of your TV if
you are assaulted by violence or offended
in some other way; call the program
director of the station. Fight air
pollution, especially for the
next generation.

*September*

26

*O*ffer to dog-sit or
plant-sit for a neighbor
who is going away.

*September*

27

*W*hen grown children leave home
to live on their own, get married or go
to college, make them a keepsake album.
Include favorite photos, awards and
newspaper clippings to let them
know they are special
and missed.

# September

## 28

*Always act in such a way that you
can look in the mirror the next morning
and like the person you see.*

— Frank McCarty

*B*e authentic. People know
if you are being phony, and they
feel closed out.

# September

**29**

*W*rite a letter of praise
to a store about a clerk or to a
school principal about
a teacher.

# September

**30**

*It may be true that the weak will always be driven to the wall, but it is the task of society to see that the wall is climbable.*

—Sidney Harris

*In* every milieu pay attention to the group as a whole; do something to include anyone who appears to feel left out.

# October

1

*You must help others.*
*If not, you should not harm others.*
—The Dalai Lama

*I*n helping others,
don't set yourself up as a critic
of those who don't.

# October

**2**

*Kids don't care what you know until they know that you care.*

— Jack Canfield

*Include children as participants in your acts of kindness; expose them to the joy of giving.*

# October

**3**

$\mathcal{B}$e kind to your environment.
Plant things, check your car exhaust,
recycle, don't waste energy
and don't litter.

# October

4

*B*e honest. Express your
feelings and your thoughts—
but don't try to impose them: Say
"I didn't like that movie," not
"That movie stinks."

## October

5

*R*espect another's fears.
However safely you may be driving,
drive more slowly if your passenger is
afraid; reassure the person who's
afraid of thunder.

## October

**6**

*Kindness is more important than wisdom,*
*and the recognition of this is the*
*beginning of wisdom.*

—Theodore Rubin

*G*ive a young person a break:
Buy those Girl Scout cookies or
give a person his first job.

# October

7

*N*ourish yourself by
associating with kind people;
be tolerant of those
who aren't.

# October

*8*

$O$ffer to help someone
who's moving; it's a dreadful task
and an emotional wrench. If you can't
lift cartons, make labels — or bring
lunch or just be supportive.

# October

9

*A*cknowledge people
with disabilities; don't act as if
they're invisible because
you're afraid.

# October

**10**

$S$uggest adopting a pet to someone who's alone—and do more: take him to an animal shelter and offer to pay for shots. Research shows that people with pets are significantly healthier.

## October

### 11

*W*rite to someone who
hasn't answered your letter;
call someone who hasn't answered
your call. Don't keep score
of who called last.

# October

## 12

*A*sk the anonymous
receptionist for her name;
make a note of it and call her by
name when you phone again.
Affirm her personhood.

*October*

*13*

*T*ake an interest in
someone's major project at work.
When you learn that it's completed,
summon the group to give him
a standing ovation.

## October

### 14

*A*sk about possible diet
restrictions of a first-time guest;
don't embarrass him by serving
something that he
can't eat.

# October

## 15

*K*eep a small towel handy
in your living room, so that if a
guest spills something, there won't
be a lot of embarrassing fuss.

*October*

16

*P*ut some postcards of
local scenes and some stamps in
your guest room.

# October

*17*

$\mathcal{G}$ive a prize for sportsmanship
in high school athletics. Two tickets to
a big college game would be nice
— not a trophy.

*October*

*18*

*W*rite your doctor a
letter of appreciation for her
spending personal time and for her
caring. Add a note to the nurse
practitioners, too!

*October*

*19*

*B*e a good neighbor.
Offer to bring in the mail and
the paper when your neighbor is on
vacation; offer to keep an
eye on his place.

# October

## 20

*C*atch someone doing it right,
and say, "Great job!"

## October

### 21

*R*emember an old neighbor
with a note saying how much you
miss her; express your appreciation of
her neighborliness and of her
friendly help.

*October*

22

*W*elcome your new neighbors with some fruit or flowers and an offer to be of help. Anticipate their needs—like knowing when the trash is collected and where the post office is; don't wait to be asked.

# October

**23**

*C*hoose not to forget your
friend's grief after the funeral is over.
Call and visit regularly. That's when
you're most needed. Invite him for
dinner and then back into life.

*October*

*24*

$\mathcal{G}$ive a party for the new
children in the neighborhood;
they need new friends.

*October*

25

_S_hare news with friends and neighbors—a "new" park, a "new" restaurant, a "new" book, a "new" discount store. You may find enjoyment of them together.

## October

**26**

$C$elebrate your Grandmother
with style. Collect little gifts all year
and give her a shopping bag full
of surprises. That's more than
a token; it's love.

# October

27

*G*et your team at work to
adopt a needy family. Get to know
the family members and to know their
needs. Then every two months
deliver a parcel—which you'll have
fun getting together to prepare.

# October

## 28

$G$ive a prize to the middle
school graduate who has written the
best poem. An anthology of poetry
might nourish a seedling talent —
or at least some future
enjoyment.

# October

*29*

$\mathcal{T}$ell a friend with enthusiasm
about someone who has given you
good service — and tell him to tell the
serviceman he was recommended.
Everybody needs recognition
for good work!

## October

**30**

*R*espect the other person's time; start your call with: "Is this a good time for you to talk?"

*October*

31

*S*uggest that everyone wear
a costume to the office on Halloween.
It's a wonderful chance to look
ridiculous—and a basis
for future fun.

# *November*

1

*R*espect the other guy's
schedule. Don't call early in the morning
or late at night unless you know he's
an early riser or goes to bed late.

# *November*

**2**

*I*n a brightly decorated box, put
a kaleidoscope and a cassette tape with
the song "Accentuate the Positive."
Write out the song's words. Give the
present to someone with a note inviting
her to look at the world through the
glorious colors of the kaleidoscope.

## November

**3**

*T*ry to enter the theatre
undramatically: on time and quietly.
Don't race out in the middle of the
curtain call—you might miss
a beautiful concert.

# *November*

*4*

*I*nvite a newly divorced friend over for dinner. Include him often in your plans and let him know he's not a "third wheel."

*November*

5

*Kind truth is honesty delivered
with compassion.*

—Sidney Simon

Commit yourself to honesty that
is compassionate and caring. Choose your
words thoughtfully when being frank
with a friend; be tactful, not blunt.

# *November*

**6**

$\mathcal{D}$evelop your own kindness
signal for communicating with loved ones.
A special whistle or sign language will
help your family reconnect in
shopping malls and other
crowded public places.

# *November*

7

*M*ake star pins to hand out
to loved ones, friends or coworkers
who have done an exceptional job. Pin the
star on their lapel, salute them, kiss
them on both cheeks and tell them
they are definitely a star.

# November

*8*

$\mathcal{T}$ake a 10-minute kindness
break today. Take a walk with someone
and only talk about good, positive things.
You'll have abundant energy for the
rest of the day and infuse
everyone around you
with good vibes.

## *November*

*9*

*W*ake up extra early and
cheerfully greet your newspaper delivery
person with a warm mug of apple cider
to go. Thank him for getting the
day's happenings to you.

# November

## 10

*P*ick up and dispose of other people's litter. And make sure to always clean up after yourself at home, work and everywhere you go. Think globally, act locally.

# *November*

**11**

*C*all or write several veterans
and thank them for their service to
the nation. Let them know their
sacrifice and courage are
still appreciated.

# *November*

*12*

*D*onate your time or money
to the local animal shelter. Most are
in need of funds, or folks to help
walk the dogs and scratch the
cats behind the ears.

## November

### 13

$\int$pread kindness around the world: send a C.A.R.E. package; support a child overseas; donate to Amnesty International; contribute to your church or synagogue's charitable outreach program; become a pen-pal.

*November*

*14*

$\mathcal{D}$o what you value and value
what you do. Make a list of your top
ten values and practice one of them today.
Intregrity is one of the greatest
gifts of kindness.

*November*

*15*

*A*sk people questions about
things you think they will enjoy talking
about. Listen attentively even if
you have heard their
stories before.

# *November*

**16**

*P*hotocopy an uplifting message
and send it to someone who could use
some spirit lifting. Keep a box of
inspirational or humorous messages and
stories on hand for those who
might need them.

*November*

*17*

*E*ncourage a beginner to try
an intelligent risk: something that
reaches the edge of his comfort level.
It will help him stretch
and grow.

# *November*

*18*

$\mathcal{P}$ut a pack of Lifesavers™ on
the desk of someone who helped you
out recently. Attach a note that
reads, "You're a lifesaver.
Thanks, a mint!"

*November*

*19*

*I*nvite your coworkers to
bring in their favorite music to the
office. The upbeat tunes will
ease the drudgery of
everyday tasks.

# November

### 20

*K*eep your connections alive.
Make an effort to regularly call a friend
or family member to see how he or she
is doing. Build these calls into
your weekly schedule.

*November*

*21*

*O*ffer encouragement for a
young person to do his or her best.
Share your experiences and
unconditional support.
Be a role model.

## *November*

**22**

*L*ook for opportunities to
validate others. Explore every chance
to show those you care about what you
admire, appreciate, respect, love and
enjoy about them. The more specific the
positive feedback, the more it
empowers them to keep up
their excellence.

# *November*

*23*

*S*eek out foreign students
who might be alone at holiday time.
Invite them to join your family
celebration. They will be interested to
learn of American traditions and
they will enjoy telling
you about theirs.

# *November*

**24**

*M*ake a list of everything you
have to be thankful for this year. If there
are special people who helped you,
write them a kind letter and let them
know of their important
role in your life.

*November*

*25*

*V*olunteer with your local
"Meals on Wheels" program. Deliver
nourishment and kindness to a
homebound elderly person.

# *November*

**26**

*P*ick up someone's newspaper
that was thrown far from her house by
mistake and deposit it on
her doorstep.

# *November*

*27*

*W*hen boarding a plane
or bus, help the mother who is
carrying her baby and all
her baby's supplies.

*November*

*28*

*L*eave an affirming message
on a friend's answering machine.
Accompany it with uplifting background
music. The next day follow up with
a silly or playful message.

*November*

29

*A*dd appreciation to your
workplace. Leave encouraging,
written validations around your office.
You'll build teamwork by tending
to human as well as
business needs.

## November

*30*

*He who laughs, lasts.*

—Mary Pettibone Poole

*B*uy a pair of Groucho
glasses for each member of your
family and have a portrait taken wearing
them. Use the portrait as a holiday
greeting card.

# December

*1*

*M*ake a commitment to providing
your customers with the absolutely top,
five-star service and attention.
Pay attention to details, listen and invest
in employee motivation. Folks will come
back to you because your place of
business makes them feel good.

# December

**2**

*B*uy your spouse a book
of love poetry. Read aloud some
selections over candlelight
and wine.

# December

*3*

*F*or no reason at all,
make up your own holiday today
to celebrate. Send a funny card
to your husband or kids.

# December

4

*R*ecycle favorite page-a-day
calendar entries by cutting off the date
and attaching a love note or affirmation.
Mail the recycled greeting to
a friend or loved one.

# *December*

5

*S*end someone on a birthday
treasure hunt. Leave clues for her with
notes attached about things you've
learned from her or admired
about her.

## December

6

*T*he next time you make
a special dish for yourself, double
the recipe. Give the extra food
to a friend or someone
in need.

## December

7

*T*ake time to talk to the
neighborhood children. Really get
to know them and be genuinely
interested in what they
have to say.

# December

*8*

*S*end a series of cards to someone for their birthday, anniversary or promotion. Sign them from famous people: "I could learn a lot about love from you. Happy Birthday— Leo Buscaglia."

# December

*9*

$\mathscr{B}$uy a stuffed animal and give
it to a friend who wants pets but can't
have them because of a busy lifestyle or a
restrictive lease. Add a note that says,
"Rover is here to greet you every
day when you come home and will
never need to be walked."

# December

### 10

$\mathcal{S}$end a humorous fax
of kindness. Keep a file of funny
quotes and cartoons relevant to your
industry and use them for
fax cover pages.

# December

*11*

*P*lan a holiday Christmas/
Hanukkah cookie-baking party for
your neighbors. Invite each person to
bring a recipe to be made in your
kitchen. Then share the goodies
with everyone.

# December

*12*

*S*hare a funny joke with someone
on a computer bulletin board.
Make sure the joke is
not offensive.

*December*

*13*

*S*end a complimentary letter to
the manufacturer of a product you like.
Let the employees know what they
produce makes a difference.

# December

*14*

*M*ake a one-minute love call.
Call a special someone you haven't
spoken with in a while just to
tell him you love him.

# December

## 15

Give yourself a standing
ovation for a job at which you've
worked especially hard. Do the
same for someone else.

# December

*16*

*L*eave special holiday gifts
for your letter carrier, newspaper
delivery person and sanitation workers.
Let them know you appreciate the
great job they've done for
you all year long.

# December

*P*ay the toll of the person
behind you at the toll booth; say,
"I'm paying for myself and my
friend in the red car
behind me."

# December

*18*

*It is when humor restores proportion
that our blind eye is open.*

—Lorraine Risly

*W*hen you are in the hospital,
spend your recovery time listening to
humorous tapes on a portable tape player
with earphones. Bliss out with laughter.

# December

*19*

*P*ay someone else's bill
at the coffee shop and leave before
she can thank you.

*December*

*20*

*A*dd "finding humor" to
your "to-do" list. When you have
found something humorous, jot it down
and review all the funny incidents at
the end of the day. Start a humor
bank and save great ideas
for the future.

# December

## 21

$G$ather your family together
and go Christmas caroling in your
neighborhood. Invite that quiet couple
who lives down the street.

# December

**22**

*S*uggest that members of
your church or synagogue write holiday
notes to shut-ins. Or visit some of the
shut-ins and suggest that they do
the writing; they may enjoy
doing it and making
new friends.

*December*

*23*

*T*ake your children to
the park and make snow angels
and build snowmen. They'll enjoy your
company and you'll rekindle the
exuberance of youth.

*December*

*24*

*W*hen planning for your
holiday dinner, purchase double
the ingredients and bring the extra to
a local hunger center. Ask them to
help a family have a great holiday, too.
Involve your children in each
step of this process.

# December

### 25

*I*nclude special notes
along with your holiday gifts.
Let the recipients know the joy
they bring to your life.

# *December*

**26**

*I*nstead of returning
presents that don't fit or you
can't use to the store, donate them
to the local homeless shelter.
Your gift will keep
on giving.

# December

**27**

$\mathcal{D}$onate your time to a
community building group
such as Habitat for Humanity.
Your efforts will provide
shelter for a
needy family.

# December

*28*

*M*ake a comfort quilt
for a sick friend. Have all her
friends design a square and sew them
together into a loving, artistic gift
that will soothe and
warm her.

# December

## 29

*M*ake it your business to remember a specific fact about your coworkers or employees. Ask questions like, "Did your mother have a nice birthday?" or "How is your son's new job?" The other person will really feel valued.

# December

**30**

*B*uy a window herb garden
kit for a friend or loved one. The edible
greenery is sure to brighten even
the dreariest winter day.

# December

*31*

*R*eview the year in a
kind frame of mind. Write down
all the positive events that happened
and make plans to build on them
in the year to come.